MW01047032

Worshiping, Working, and Waiting

(Insights for Daily Living from First Thessalonians)

THOMAS R. HENDERSHOT

Unless otherwise indicated, all scripture is from the World English Bible (WEB). The World English Bible (WEB) is a Public Domain (no copyright) Modern English translation of the Holy Bible. The WEB is annotated throughout this book when I have listed a passage with more than one translation together.

Other Versions used are:

Scripture quotations noted AMP are taken from the Amplified® Bible, Copyright © 1954, 1958, 1962, 1964, 1965, 1987 by The Lockman Foundation. Used by permission. (www.Lockman.org).

Scripture quotations marked (ESV) are from the Holy Bible, English Standard Version ® (ESV), copyright 2001 by Crossway Bibles, a publishing ministry of Good News Publishers. Used by permission. All rights reserved.

Scripture quotations marked (KJV) are from the King James Version.

Scripture marked (MEV) is taken from the Modern English Version, Copyright © 2014 by Military Bible Association. Used by permission. All rights reserved.

Scripture quotations marked (NASB) are taken from the NEW AMERICAN STANDARD BIBLE®, Copyright © 1960, 1962, 1963, 1968, 1971, 1972, 1973, 1975, 1977, 1995 by The Lockman Foundation. Used by permission."

Scripture quotations marked (NKJV) are taken from the New King James Version® (NKJV), Copyright © 1982 by Thomas Nelson, Inc. Used by permission. All rights reserved.

DEDICATION

To David

WORSHIPING, WORKING, AND WAITING

CONTENTS

WORSHIPING, WORKING, AND WAITING

INTRODUCTION

The Apostle Paul began this letter, which is likely the first he wrote to a church which we have a record of, with thanksgiving, comments about their work of faith and labor of love and words expressing the early church's expectation of the return of Jesus. As one reads the letter, we can see the theme emerge of worshiping, working and waiting.

Paul commended these believers for the way in which they lived their faith. They had become a model church for others to emulate. Finding a proper balance and expression of these three areas of Christian life is a key to living a life that is pleasing to God and an example to others.

Paul said many things in this letter that fit the premise of encouraging believers to develop a lifestyle of worship. He told them to rejoice, to pray, to prophesy, and to give thanks. Throughout, his theme of encouraging believers to walk properly before the Lord in the world while doing the work they were called to do is evident. Also in this epistle, Paul shared one of the clearest passages given in the entire Bible about the second coming of Jesus. It is a beautiful text that informed of what they needed to know about Christ's return in a simple way, yet with profound imagery. These believers were waiting for Jesus to come again. This text of Christ's return was an encouraging word of truth for them.

I am convinced that the Bible is not merely a history book. I do not believe it is just the record of previous encounters between God and humans. I believe it is the living Word of God and is meant to be read and applied to our daily lives and our current time. In the following pages, we shall briefly explore some of the blessed truths of this letter in small devotional segments seeking to apply what Paul said to them by inspiration of the Holy Spirit to our modern lives.

"May God bless us to grow in His grace and in the knowledge of our Lord and Savior, Jesus Christ" (Acts 6:4, 2 Pet. 3:8). Amen!

1

EXAMPLES

DAY ONE: "Getting Started."

Today let's familiarize ourselves with chapter one of First Thessalonians. In this chapter, Paul emphasized the great example the believers in Thessalonica were to everyone who knew them or heard about them. We can certainly learn a lot from reading this chapter and should carefully apply its truth to our lives. Let's make this our goal as we go forward.

CLOSING WORD: **"¹Paul, Silvanus, and Timothy, to the assembly of the Thessalonians in God the Father and the Lord Jesus Christ: Grace to you and peace from God our Father and the Lord Jesus Christ. ²We always give thanks to God for all of you, mentioning you in our prayers, ³ remembering without ceasing your work of faith and labor of love and patience of hope in our Lord Jesus Christ, before our God and Father. ⁴We know, brothers loved by God, that you are chosen, ⁵ and that our Good News came to you not in word only, but also in power, and in the Holy Spirit, and with much assurance. You know what kind** of men we showed ourselves to be among you for your sake. [6]You became imitators of us, and of the Lord, having received the word in much affliction, with joy of the Holy Spirit, [7] so that you became an example to all who believe in Macedonia and in Achaia. [8]For from you the word of the Lord has been declared, not only in Macedonia and Achaia, but also in every place your faith toward God has gone out; so that we need not to say anything. [9]For they themselves report concerning us what kind of a reception we had from you; and how you turned to God from idols, to serve a living and true God, [10] and to wait for his Son from heaven, whom he raised from the dead—Jesus, who delivers us from the wrath to come." (1 Thessalonians 1:1-10, WEB)

PRAYER: "Our Father, as we begin this exciting journey through this short letter of Paul written to a church many years ago, help us to hear what Your Holy Spirit is speaking to us today. Open our eyes to see the truth You have for us to see. Open our minds to comprehend Your instruction to us. Open our hearts to commit our lives afresh to You in complete obedience. We ask these things through the Lord Jesus Christ. Amen."

DAY TWO: "Receiving the Grace and Peace of God."

"Grace to you and peace from God our Father and the Lord Jesus Christ" (1:1b). Let's receive the grace and peace of God. Grace and peace come to us from God the Father through His Son. Some folks never pursue a relationship with God because they feel they are not "good enough" to have one. Their assumption is correct, we are not. However, we may have a vibrant relationship with the living God. Why? The answer is because a relationship with God is based on His grace, not our goodness! This relationship is the grace of God.

God initiates this relationship. Grace is the opposite of what we deserve. It is the unmerited favor of God. We can never earn the blessings of God. We cannot do enough of the "right stuff" to merit

His favor. Grace means, "God favors us freely." Our response must be to receive what He offers freely to us. However, we must respond to God in order to receive all of the blessings He has for us. He draws us to a response and empowers us to respond. This is grace.

Peace can be described as the relationship we now enjoy because we are no longer the enemies of God. God has come to us in grace and freely offers us complete forgiveness of our sins and the privilege to walk in right relationship with Him. This right relationship brings peace to every area of our lives.

In what areas of your life is there turmoil? Where can you recognize your need for the peace of God? Ask Him to show you how you can let His peace operate powerfully in your heart and mind in every area of your life.

CLOSING WORD: **"⁶In nothing be anxious, but in everything, by prayer and petition with thanksgiving, let your requests be made known to God. ⁷And the peace of God, which surpasses all understanding, will guard your hearts and your thoughts in Christ Jesus."** (Philippians 4:6-7)

PRAYER: "Our Father, I come to You now thanking You for Your grace in my life. You have given to me the very opposite of what I deserved. You continue to do this in my life. I thank You for forgiving my sin and giving me a new life to live now. I ask You to show me every area of my life where I have not fully surrendered to You and allowed Your peace to reign supremely. I give You these issues and items today. (Name some things that come into your heart and mind as you wait now before Him). Dear Lord, keep me in peace as I trust in You. I ask this through Jesus Christ, Your Son, my Lord. Amen."

DAY THREE: "Cultivating a Lifestyle of Thanksgiving."

"²We always give thanks to God for all of you, mentioning you in

3

our prayers, ³ **remembering without ceasing your work of faith and labor of love and patience of hope in our Lord Jesus Christ, before our God and Father."** (1:2-3)

We should often tell others we appreciate them. Paul told these believers that he and his team were thankful for them. He set a wonderful example here for us to follow. He expressed his thankfulness to them. He even wrote them a letter and publicly acknowledged how thankful he was for them. It was an important thing to do. It was the right thing to do. I am sure this meant a lot to them. It would mean a lot to some folks we know too. Therefore, thank God for others in your life. Notice, Paul prayed for these folks. We should also pray for others and thank God for them in our prayers and with many other ways.

We should be thankful at all times and for all things. Thanksgiving is essential in our worship. It is the right attitude for us to have toward God. It will change the way we look at life. Later in this same letter Paul encouraged them with these words: "**In everything give thanks, for this is the will of God in Christ Jesus toward you."** (5:18) Doing this will change your attitude about God, about your situations, about the other people in your life, and it will brighten your day. It is the right and necessary perspective for us to have.

CLOSING WORD: "**¹I exhort therefore, first of all, that petitions, prayers, intercessions, and giving of thanks, be made for all men: ² for kings and all who are in high places; that we may lead a tranquil and quiet life in all godliness and reverence. ³For this is good and acceptable in the sight of God our Savior; ⁴ who desires all people to be saved and come to full knowledge of the truth."** (1 Timothy 2:1-4)

PRAYER: "Our Father, I thank You today for all of the wonderful people You have put into my life. I ask You to bless them all. Bring those who do not know You into a right relationship with You. Help me to be more thankful for each of them. Show me ways to express my thanks to them. I ask this in Your holy name, Amen."

DAY FOUR: "Recognizing God's Word is Active and Produces Fruit."

Jesus said His Word was like the seed scattered on the ground that will produce a harvest (Mark 4:14). The Word of God produces a harvest. It brought these folks the good news of the grace and peace of God. It worked in their lives bringing forth fruit. "**...remembering without ceasing your work of faith and labor of love and patience of hope in our Lord Jesus Christ, before our God and Father.**" (1:3)

It strengthened their faith. "**⁴ We know, brothers loved by God, that you are chosen, ⁵ and that our Good News came to you not in word only, but also in power, and in the Holy Spirit, and with much assurance.**" (4-5a)

It produced faithfulness in their lives. Take a moment and read again verses 5b-10 above at the beginning of this chapter.

Notice the Word caused them to become examples of faith to others:

1. As individuals. The life they lived before each other impacted one another. It always does. We are affected, and we affect (sometimes infect) those around us.

2. As a body of believers. The whole church was a model for other churches to follow. They set a wonderful example of faith.

Ask yourself: What kind of an example do I set that others can model? What kind of an example does the church body I belong to set that others should follow?

CLOSING WORD: "**¹³You are the salt of the earth, but if the salt has lost its flavor, with what will it be salted? It is then good for nothing, but to be cast out and trodden under the feet of men. ¹⁴You are the light of the world. A city located on a hill can't be hidden. ¹⁵Neither do you light a lamp, and put it under a measuring basket, but on a stand; and it shines to all who are in the house. ¹⁶Even so, let your light shine before men; that they may see your good works, and glorify your**

Father who is in heaven." (Matthew 5:13-16)

PRAYER: "O' Lord, let Your Word be active and fruitful within me and in my life. Change me through Your Word and Spirit and make me more like Jesus. Let my life be an example to those who are watching me. In Your name, I ask You for this, Amen."

DAY FIVE: "Things that Should Accompany the Word."

"And that our Good News came to you not in word only, but also in power, and in the Holy Spirit, and with much assurance." (Vs. 5)

I stand for and stand upon the Word of God. We are saved because of the truth we hear and believe. This is God's method. He uses His Word to save us (Romans 10:14-17). The Bible preserves this message of truth that reveals His salvation. It tells us of our need for God and how He calls us into a relationship with Himself. We should say with David, **"Your word is a lamp to my feet, and a light for my path"** (Psalm 119:105). His Word is good. It is necessary. It is vital. It brings life to us. It explains what His Spirit does in us. The Good News comes to us through His Word.

However, there should be things that accompany the Word. The true gospel which they had received was not just talk. It came in power, it came in the Holy Spirit, and it brought much assurance. These things accompanied the Word. All of these aspects were the work of the Holy Spirit in their lives through God's Word. We need the presence and ministry of the Holy Spirit too. Without this, the Word can be misapplied and misused. Without this, our faith might be based on the most convincing speaker rather than on the truth. Folks can be effective public speakers and not even know Christ (Matthew 7:23, 1 Corinthians 2:4, Galatians 1:7-8, Philippians 1:15). However, this is not true gospel preaching. True gospel messengers are Spirit-empowered messengers. Anything less than Spirit-empowered preaching is not true gospel preaching. Quoting the Bible is not enough. Folks can quote scriptures and also be downright hateful at the same time. That is the dead letter. The saving gospel is the Word used and applied to our lives by the Holy Spirit. This brings eternal life to us. It causes transformation. It gives us real assurance. This is true worship.

The truth is not in Word only. It is also in the power of the Holy Spirit and much assurance. Ask God to make His truth real to you. By His power, He makes the truth a reality in our lives. Don't settle for the dead letter of religion. Respond to God and experience the living Christ of the real gospel.

CLOSING WORD: "**[23]But the hour comes, and now is, when the true worshipers will worship the Father in spirit and truth, for the Father seeks such to be his worshipers. [24] God is spirit, and those who worship him must worship in spirit and truth.**" (John 4:23-24)

PRAYER: "Father, I believe this is the time, this is the hour in which I can know You. Deliver me from dead religion. I do not want to have the Word without the Spirit also. Help me to know You in truth. Help me to experience the Good News of Jesus in Your power, in the Holy Spirit, and in much assurance. Bring me into a new reality of knowing You as I have never experienced before. I believe You are alive. Be alive in me. In the Name of Jesus Christ, the Lord, I ask this. Amen."

DAY SIX: "Learning to Recognize a Model Church or Model Believer and Follow Their Example."

The following is what it looked like at the church at Thessalonica. They were a thankful people. Their lives modeled this grateful attitude (vs. 1-3). They knew they were a chosen people. They knew this and acted like they were God's favorite kids (vs. 4). This spiritual knowledge was not arrogance. It was an assurance from God. It was an understanding of grace. They were saved because God had chosen them to believe. They knew that God had chosen them to worship, work and wait.

A genuine realization that God chooses one to follow Him inspires true heartfelt worship from the depths of the soul. The knowledge of their election was a definite reason for their thankful attitudes. It inspires a person to work for the Kingdom of God. It encourages a person to wait for the Son of God to return. It gives purpose for this life and hope for the life to come.

Therefore, Paul reminded them of this truth. It motivated them to do good works and model their faith in front of others. Below, let's look further at some definite ways in which they were a model church.

1. They were also a powerful people (vs. 5). They were powerful:

A. In the Word of God.

B. In the Holy Spirit.

C. In their assurance (much assurance).

2. They were a witnessing people (esp. vs. 8):

A. By their words (testimony).

B. By their example(s). They continued in assurance in their faith during affliction (Vs. 6).

C. By their joy. Their deep joy during affliction was a testimony of their faith.

3. They were an expectant people (vs. 10). They were always looking for Jesus to come onto the scene at any minute and make His presence known.

Below are seven important questions we should ask ourselves based off of this text:

1. Am I truly a thankful person?

2. Are others thankful for me?

3. Do I honestly believe that I am one of God's chosen people?

4. Do I believe in and express the power of God in Word, in Spirit, and in His assurance?

5. Do I tell others through my words and deeds about my faith?

6. Do others report well about my faith and joy? (vs. 9)

7. Do I live in an expectation of Christ's activity in my life? (vs. 10)

CLOSING WORD: "⁹But you are a chosen race, a royal priesthood, a holy nation, a people for God's own possession, that you may proclaim the excellence of him who called you out of darkness into his marvelous light: ¹⁰ who in time past were no people, but now are God's people, who had not obtained mercy, but now have obtained mercy. ¹¹Beloved, I beg you as foreigners and pilgrims, to abstain from fleshly lusts, which war against the soul; ¹² having good behavior among the nations, so in that of which they speak against you as evildoers, they may by your good works, which they see, glorify God in the day of visitation" (1 Peter 2:9-12).

PRAYER: "O' Lord, open my eyes to see the positive examples You have put into my life for me to follow. Help me to be honest with myself and rise up to be the person You have called me to be in my generation. In the Name of Christ Jesus, the Lord, I ask this. Amen."

DAY SEVEN: "They Participated in the Ministry" (v. 8).

In another place, Paul told certain believers that they were "living letters" (2 Corinthians 3:2). The same thing is true with us too. People are reading our lives regardless of the words we use. Paul mentioned the Thessalonians', "work of faith and labor of love and patience of hope in our Lord Jesus Christ, before our God and Father." (vs. 3)

People are watching us. Are we living a life that displays faith, hope, and love? These believers had a lifestyle of faith, not just a profession of faith. Paul says our life should progress from "faith to faith." They also maintained faith during their sufferings. In their case, it was not just what others said when things were going well that made such an impact on the observers. There was something more. They possessed a deep stability that we all also need. They had learned to suffer successfully. They had spiritual assurance in affliction. They saw the bigger picture by faith (2 Corinthians 4:16-17). They had a lifestyle of thanksgiving. It was infectious to others in a positive way. They were a witnessing community. They labored in love for others. It is no small wonder that they had such a good reputation. They were believers who were fully committed to God and in love with Jesus Christ. They were in love with God and each other, and it showed. They participated in the ministry. They were not just holy observers. They were participants. They left an example worth following.

CLOSING WORD: **"But now faith, hope, and love remain—these three. The greatest of these is love"** (1 Corinthians 13:13)

PRAYER: "Dear Father, take me. Take me, break me, and make me all over again into the image of Jesus. Then give the new me (filled with Christ) to the world around me. Help me to not be conformed to the image of this world that puts self-interest ahead of everything else. Mold me into the image of Jesus. Let others see the love of Jesus through my life. Manifest His goodness through me in all that I say and do. In the precious name of Jesus, I ask this. Amen."

DAY EIGHT: "Do the Work of Your Ministry."

"For from you the word of the Lord has been declared, not only in Macedonia and Achaia, but also in every place your faith toward God has gone out; so that we need not to say anything." (vs. 8)

There is a work to faith. It is not all just mental assent or intellectual believing. It involves action too (James 1:22, 2:20-21). Make no mistake about it, the *easy-believism* of the modern culture is not the faith of the Bible. God has a work for you to do (Eph. 2:10).

Paul commended these believers for their, "work of faith and labor of love." They were active in their faith. They were not sitting around saying, "whatever God has predestined to happen, will happen." They believed they were a part of God's predestined plan and got themselves busy doing it. They lived their faith for all to see.

In what area is God calling you to become more active? For whom is God leading you to pray? To whom is God speaking to you to talk with about their eternal destiny? How can you make a difference where you are? How can you help in your church? Don't just sit around wishing and waiting for something to happen. Let's get busy and put our faith to work. Let's put some labor into our love.

CLOSING WORD: "**⁷Beloved, let us love one another, for love is of God; and everyone who loves has been born of God, and knows God. ⁸He who doesn't love doesn't know God, for God is love.**" (1 John 4:7-8)

PRAYER: "Dear Father, I repent for not being as active as I should have been. Forgive me. Please don't allow my friends and family to miss out on Your blessings because I did not do what I should have done. Use me, O' Lord. Cause Your love to motivate me to get busy in Your kingdom. Compel me with Your compassion to do what You have called me to do in this time. I ask this in Your holy name. Amen."

DAY NINE: "The Word Produces Results."

"**⁹For they themselves report concerning us what kind of a reception we had from you; and how you turned to God from idols, to serve a living and true God, ¹⁰ and to wait for his Son from heaven, whom he raised from the dead—Jesus, who delivers us from the wrath to come.**" (Vs. 9-10)

The promise that Christ would return was a foundational belief of the early church (Acts 1:11). They were a people of hope. They were waiting for Jesus to come back and for the resurrection. However, this did not stop them from actively worshiping and working. Belief that Christ will return mustn't deter us from being busy for His kingdom while we wait for His return. These are some fundamental traits of genuine Christianity: We worship; we work, and we wait.

It goes back to the theological virtues of faith, hope and love. The true believers have faith. They worship because they believe. God has given them faith to believe. Therefore, they worship. However, it is a living faith that is alive with activity (James 1:22, 2:18). They are doers of the work (James 1:25). They have the love of God in their hearts. Consequently, they work the works of God for others around them. They possess the hope that comes from heaven. Therefore, they wait patiently and actively for Christ's return. When believers live this way, it causes others to take note. Others see the hope within them (1 Peter 3:15). Word gets around.

CLOSING WORD: **"Wait for Yahweh. Be strong, and let your heart take courage. Yes, wait for Yahweh."** (Psalm 27:14)

PRAYER: "O' LORD, teach me to wait for You. You are sovereign. Your reign is supreme. You are my Lord and my God. My times are in Your hands. Help me to worship You as I should and stay busy for Your cause as I wait for You to come again. In the name of the King, who has come and is coming again, Jesus, I ask this. Amen."

DAY TEN: "The Word in Action."

THE WORD FOR TODAY: **"²²Be doers of the word and not hearers only, deceiving yourselves. ²³For if anyone is a hearer of the word and not a doer, he is like a man viewing his natural face in a mirror. ²⁴ He views himself, and goes his way, and immediately forgets what kind of man he was. ²⁵But whoever looks into the perfect law of liberty, and**

continues in it, and is not a forgetful hearer but a doer of the work, this man will be blessed in his deeds." (James 1:22-25, MEV)

Let's put love into our labor. Otherwise, the labor might be short-lived and will certainly not bring forth the results it should. One of the leading causes of burn-out in church work is from folks laboring with the wrong motivation. Love for God and our neighbor must be our driving dynamic.

In the spaces below, consider how meditating and praying through this section of the Word of God has changed your life. Write some bullet-statements on the next page as you consider how God is transforming you through His Word and Spirit. I have provided a couple examples to help you get started. These can certainly take on any form for each individual. Ask God to help you to see how He wants to apply the truth of this passage to your life. Begin to prepare an action plan.

PRAYER: "O' LORD God, help me now to see the areas where You desire for me to increase in faith and grow in the work of the gospel and the kingdom. Guide me as I contemplate this issues at hand. I ask this in Jesus' name. Amen."

How I Will Apply the Truth in my Daily Life:

My Work of Faith:

(*Example) I am going to start helping with Sunday School at my church.

_____

_____

_____

_____

_____

_____

_____

_____

_____

_____

_____

_____

_____

_____

_____

_____

_____

_____

_____

_____

_____

_____

My Labor of Love:

* I really enjoying helping in (   ) ministry.   I am going to...

_____

_____

_____

_____

_____

_____

_____

_____

_____

_____

_____

_____

_____

_____

_____
_____
_____
_____
_____

My Confident Expectation:

* I refuse to worry about (_____) any longer.   I commit
this situation into God's hands and will trust Him with the results.

_____
_____
_____
_____
_____
_____
_____
_____
_____
_____
_____
_____
_____
_____
_____
_____
_____
_____
_____
_____
_____
_____
_____
_____

THOMAS R. HENDERSHOT

2

ENEMIES AND ENTHUSIASTS

DAY ELEVEN: "Chapter Two."

Today let's familiarize ourselves with chapter two of First Thessalonians. In this chapter, Paul tells about some of the enemies of his and his companions. These folks opposed the Good News preached by Paul and his team. There were also many who believed his message and were enthusiastic followers of Jesus and Paul (1 Corinthians 11:1). We can discover vital truth from reading this chapter carefully and applying it to our lives. Let's make this our goal as we go forward in chapter two of this wonderful letter.

CLOSING WORD: **"¹For you yourselves know, brothers, our visit to you wasn't in vain, ²but having suffered before and been shamefully treated, as you know, at Philippi, we grew bold in our God to tell you the Good News of God in much conflict. ³For our exhortation is not of error, nor of uncleanness, nor in deception. ⁴But even as we have been approved by God to be entrusted with the Good News, so we speak; not as pleasing men, but God, who tests our hearts. ⁵For neither were we** at any time found using words of flattery, as you know, nor a cloak of covetousness (God is witness), ⁶ nor seeking glory from men (neither from you nor from others), when we might have claimed authority as apostles of Christ. ⁷But we were gentle among you, like a nursing mother cherishes her own children. ⁸Even so, affectionately longing for you, we were well pleased to impart to you, not the Good News of God only, but also our own souls, because you had become very dear to us. ⁹For you remember, brothers, our labor and travail; for working night and day, that we might not burden any of you, we preached to you the Good News of God. ¹⁰You are witnesses with God, how holy, righteously, and blamelessly we behaved ourselves toward you who believe. ¹¹As you know, we exhorted, comforted, and implored every one of you, as a father does his own children, ¹² to the end that you should walk worthily of God, who calls you into his own Kingdom and glory. ¹³For this cause we also thank God without ceasing, that, when you received from us the word of the message of God, you accepted it not as the word of men, but, as it is in truth, the word of God, which also works in you who believe. ¹⁴For you, brothers, became imitators of the assemblies of God which are in Judea in Christ Jesus; for you also suffered the same things from your own countrymen, even as they did from the Jews; ¹⁵ who killed both the Lord Jesus and their own prophets, and drove us out, and didn't please God, and are contrary to all men; ¹⁶ forbidding us to speak to the Gentiles that they may be saved; to fill up their sins always. But wrath has come on them to the uttermost. ¹⁷But we, brothers, being bereaved of you for a short season, in presence, not in heart, tried even harder to see your face with great desire, ¹⁸ because we wanted to come to you—indeed, I, Paul, once and again—but Satan hindered us. ¹⁹For what is our hope, or joy, or crown of rejoicing? Isn't it even you, before our Lord Jesus at his coming? ²⁰For you are our glory and our joy." (1 Thessalonians 2:1-20)

PRAYER: "Our Father, as we begin learning about the truth of this chapter and applying it to our lives help us to hear what Your Holy Spirit is speaking to us today and the days ahead. As we did at the beginning of chapter one, again we ask You to open our eyes to see the truth You have for us to see in this chapter. Open our minds to comprehend Your instruction to us. Open our hearts to commit our lives afresh to You in complete obedience. We ask these things through the Lord Jesus Christ. Amen."

DAY TWELVE: "Pushing Back with Spiritual Confidence."

"**¹For you yourselves know, brothers, our visit to you wasn't in vain, ²but having suffered before and been shamefully treated, as you know, at Philippi, we grew bold in our God to tell you the Good News of God in much conflict."** (2:1-2)

It is easy for us to make it all about ourselves. When we endeavor to help others, we have a certain expectation that everything will go well. After all, we surmise, if we are doing this for God then it should have that "divine flow" to it. Right? However, this is often not the case. In general, there is resistance of various sorts. Things going along without problems is not the sure sign of divine approval. Often, we will meet with resistance as we try to help others in the gospel way. There is always that crowd on the sideline saying, "If this is of God it will not have any opposition." That is simply not the truth.

Paul and his company, however, did not let the problems they had endured earlier in Philippi sour their ministry in Thessalonica. Rather, they used it as a source to embolden their testimony. They persevered against the opposition. Paul refused to allow resistance and opposition to define the truth he proclaimed or the ministry he presented.

We also must learn not to allow resistance and opposition to define who we are in God and what we have to say about Jesus. Our ministry is in vain if we allow the opposition to define it. We must leave the results with God. My friend, Dr. Terry Downin, has often reminded me that the Lord's words still are, "You proclaim, I'll persuade!" Let's do our part and leave the rest to God.

CLOSING WORD: **"I have told you these things, that in me you may have peace. In the world you have oppression; but cheer up! I have overcome the world."** (John 16:33)

PRAYER: "Our Father, help me today to not view difficulties as proof that Your Word is not going forward into the places You have sent me to proclaim it. I submit my life and work to You. Give me confidence that my work for You is not in vain. Give me boldness to continue every good work You have called me to do and to expect fruit. In Jesus' name! Amen"

DAY THIRTEEN: "Personally Convinced."

"For you yourselves know,....." (2:1a)

Our spiritual boldness and confidence increases when we become personally convinced that something is right (Proverbs 28:1). Spiritual boldness is lacking in our day. We are constantly told that truth is relative. We are bombarded with the idea that there are many truths and no one right way. However, this is not the view of God and the Bible. In the scripture, truth is absolute (John 8:32). Truth is a Person. Therefore, knowing the truth and being convinced in our own mind involves personally knowing this Person, who is the ultimate Truth. If we are not convinced of the truth, it could be a sign that we do not actually know the One who is the Truth as we should. We should often check this in our mind and experience (2 Corinthians 13:5). With the truth comes assurance. "May God convince each of us today!"

CLOSING WORD: **"Jesus said to him, "I am the way, the truth, and the life."** (John 14:6a)

PRAYER: "Dear Lord Jesus, I call upon You today. I acknowledge that You are the ultimate Truth of the universe. I also realize that I am a sinner and that unless You reveal Yourself to me I can never truly know You or experience Your reality. I come to You now asking You to open my eyes to the Truth and convince me of Your reality. In Your holy name, I pray. Amen."

DAY FOURTEEN: "Pure Motives."

"For our exhortation is not of error, nor of uncleanness, nor in deception." (2:3)

Paul is not saying God's messengers are perfect or need to be totally sinless. Jesus Christ is the only sinless one who ever walked this earth. However, Paul is saying that our attitudes and motives do matter. There is a place in this where we harvest what we have planted. We do not reap a harvest of salvation when we have scattered seeds that are not the truth about salvation. We should be careful what we are saying to people and what they believe based off of our words (2 Timothy 2:15, James 3:1).

Paul was certain that his motives and methods were right. I think that is amazing. His intentions were pure. He had no desire to deceive them. He wanted to communicate only the truth to them. Let us ask God to give us the right motives and attitudes to effectively minister grace to those around us.

CLOSING WORD: "³Who may ascend to Yahweh's hill? Who may stand in his holy place? ⁴He who has clean hands and a pure heart; who has not lifted up his soul to falsehood, and has not sworn deceitfully. ⁵He shall receive a blessing from Yahweh, righteousness from the God of his salvation. ⁶This is the generation of those who seek Him, who seek your face—even Jacob. Selah." (Psalm 24:3-6)

PRAYER: "Father God, help each of us to be right with You and right with those around us. Help us to have no selfish or self-centered motives for what we do for You and for others. Give us pure hearts, clean thoughts, and sincere spirits. In Jesus' Name. Amen."

DAY FIFTEEN: "The Difference Between Leading and Pushing."

"³For our exhortation is not of error, nor of uncleanness, nor in deception. ⁴But even as we have been approved by God to be entrusted with the Good News, so we speak; not as pleasing men, but God, who tests our hearts. ⁵For neither were we at any time found using words of flattery, as you know, nor a cloak of covetousness (God is witness), ⁶nor seeking glory from men (neither from you nor from others), when we might have claimed authority as apostles of Christ." (2:4-6)

Most of us, today do not like the feeling that someone is pushing us. This sentiment is especially applicable in the religious settings in our time. Some have the impression that their parents or others "pushed" religion on them during their childhood. Some still deeply resent this. Folks have been driven away from church or have rebelled because of these feelings. Regardless of the reality of someone's experience, it is still their opinion. It influences their beliefs and actions.

In regard to spiritual things, this is not an easy terrain. Parents have a Biblical responsibility to raise their kids in the faith. However, the same methods do not always work in every case. We would be wise to recognize this.

In general, the shepherds of old led the sheep. The sheep followed their shepherd. Usually, they did not drive them as one would cattle, for instance. I am convinced that different situations require different strategies at times. However, often the best method for ministering to others, especially in our time and culture, is by leading. We must trust that the Lord will call His own to follow Him faithfully. We are under-shepherds. He is the Chief Shepherd (1 Peter 5:4). If we find ourselves driving the sheep often, we should probably check our motives and methods.

CLOSING WORD: **"¹⁴ I am the good shepherd. I know my own, and I'm known by my own; ¹⁵ even as the Father knows me, and I know the Father. I lay down my life for the sheep."** (John 10:14-15)

PRAYER: *"²⁰Now may the God of peace, who brought again from the dead the great shepherd of the sheep with the blood of an eternal covenant, our Lord Jesus, ²¹ make you complete in every good work to do his will, working in you that which is well pleasing in his sight, through Jesus Christ, to whom be the glory forever and ever. Amen."* (Hebrews 13:20-21).

DAY SIXTEEN: "Relying on God, Not Trendy Methods."

"For neither were we at any time found using words of flattery, as you know, nor a cloak of covetousness (God is witness),..." (2:5)

Folks resort to every imaginable method to gain followers now as then. Not so for Paul. Why do modern leaders rely on everything other than the Word and Spirit? For several possible reasons. Let's consider a few.

Sometimes it is a result of contention (vs. 3). Other times, it is because of deceit, impure motives, or simply trying to get something from others. Some folks believe that the presence of God is subject to the right lighting, music, or some methods of trickery. Paul did not travel with a band. Paul used no tricks. He was pure in his intentions, and God used him greatly.

Certainly, the atmosphere is important when we worship. Music, when used, obviously matters. However, we must be careful with our intentions. We should not automatically run after the newest fad. God is not dependent on man's methods. Talent is important, but holiness is much more important. Skill is great, but the anointing is better. Let's not rely on human tactics and techniques. God method is the Word, and the Spirit (Isaiah 39:1, Jeremiah 17:5, Zechariah 4:6).

CLOSING WORD: **"It is the spirit who gives life. The flesh profits nothing. The words that I speak to you are spirit, and are life."** (John 6:63)

PRAYER: "Our Father, teach us to trust You and not in our methods. Lord Jesus, give us the right motives and attitudes. Holy Spirit, purge our thoughts and minds by Your Word and by Your presence. Amen."

DAY SEVENTEEN: "What Makes the Word Work?"

"For this cause we also thank God without ceasing, that, when you received from us the word of the message of God, you accepted it not as the word of men, but, as it is in truth, the word of God, which also works in you who believe." (2:13)

We must receive the truth for it to do its work within us. We are sinners by nature. God brings His truth to us. We must receive it and let it change us. Hearing it is not enough. Many folks hear it and never allow it to change them. They do not have faith. God gives His children faith to receive the truth and be changed by it. Some folks try to resist any change. There is never peace and blessing in our lives until we submit to God's ways. When we receive the Word, it produces results in our lives. They who receive it also receive the benefits of its life-giving power. Accept all that God is speaking into your life now. Expect changes to happen in your life as you believe His Word.

CLOSING WORD: **"If you abide in My word, you are My disciples indeed. 32And you shall know the truth, and the truth shall make you free."** (John 8:31b-32)

PRAYER: "Our Father, we give You thanks that You have given us faith to believe You and the spiritual ability to hear Your Words. Grant that we may continue in Your Word and be changed more and more into the image of Your Son, for its in His name we ask. Amen."

DAY EIGHTEEN: "Opposition."

"**Because we wanted to come to you—indeed, I, Paul, once and again—but Satan hindered us.**" (2:18)

Smooth seas do not result in producing skilled sailors. Character is formed in the wilderness. We must expect opposition. We should not be discouraged when we have trouble on this pathway. The devil also has an agenda. However, God is greater than the devil.

We acknowledge the presence of evil in this world. We expect opposition from it. We should not be ignorant of the devices of the devil. We should be sober and watchful. We should guard our hearts and minds. We must stay full of the Word and the Spirit. We must keep our hearts right with God and man.

CLOSING WORD: "**Therefore submit yourselves to God. Resist the devil, and he will flee from you.**" (James 4:7)

PRAYER: "Our Lord and God, we thank You that You always cause us to triumph through Jesus Christ. Therefore, we resist evil and submit ourselves to You. Keep us safe and keep us in the righteousness of Jesus Christ, as it is in His name we ask this. Amen."

DAY NINETEEN: "The Word in Action."

THE WORD FOR TODAY: "**²Grace to you, and peace from God, our Father, and the Lord Jesus Christ. ³I thank my God whenever I remember you, ⁴ always in every request of mine on behalf of you all making my requests with joy, ⁵ for your partnership in furtherance of the Good News from the first day until now; ⁶ being confident of this very thing, that he who began a good work in you will complete it until the day of Jesus Christ.**" (Philippians 1:2-6)

PRAYER: "O' Lord, I know I cannot be the person You would have me to be nor do the things You want me to do without the help of Your Holy Spirit. Help me now to apply the truth I have seen in this chapter to my life as You see fit. In Your name, I ask. Amen."

How I Will Apply the Truth in my Daily Life:

Worshiping God:

_____

_____

_____

_____

_____

_____

_____

_____

_____

_____

_____

_____

_____

_____

_____

_____

_____

_____

_____

_____

_____

_____

_____

_____

_____

Working for God:

_____

_____

_____

_____

_____
_____
_____
_____
_____
_____
_____
_____
_____
_____
_____
_____
_____

Waiting on God:
_____
_____
_____
_____
_____
_____
_____
_____
_____
_____
_____
_____
_____
_____
_____
_____
_____

THOMAS R. HENDERSHOT

3

ENCOURAGEMENT

DAY TWENTY: "Chapter Three."

Today let's familiarize ourselves with chapter three of First Thessalonians. In this chapter, Paul tells about some of his discouraging times and how God used these folks to encourage him. We can trust He will do the same for us. I trust we will uncover some encouraging words from reading this chapter carefully and applying it to our lives. Let's make this our goal as we go forward with chapter three now.

CLOSING WORD: **"¹Therefore when we couldn't stand it any longer, we thought it good to be left behind at Athens alone, ² and sent Timothy, our brother and God's servant in the Good News of Christ, to establish you, and to comfort you concerning your faith; ³ that no one be moved by these afflictions. For you know that we are appointed to this task. ⁴ For most certainly, when we were with you, we told you beforehand that we are to suffer affliction, even as it happened, and you know. ⁵ For this cause I also, when I couldn't stand it any longer,**

---

sent that I might know your faith, for fear that by any means the tempter had tempted you, and our labor would have been in vain. [6]But when Timothy came just now to us from you, and brought us glad news of your faith and love, and that you have good memories of us always, longing to see us, even as we also long to see you; [7]for this cause, brothers, we were comforted over you in all our distress and affliction through your faith. [8]For now we live, if you stand fast in the Lord. [9]For what thanksgiving can we render again to God for you, for all the joy with which we rejoice for your sakes before our God; [10]night and day praying exceedingly that we may see your face, and may perfect that which is lacking in your faith? [11]Now may our God and Father himself, and our Lord Jesus Christ, direct our way to you; [12]and the Lord make you to increase and abound in love one toward another, and toward all men, even as we also do toward you, [13]to the end he may establish your hearts blameless in holiness before our God and Father, at the coming of our Lord Jesus with all his saints." (1 Thessalonians 3:1-13)

PRAYER: "Our Father, as we begin learning about the truth of chapter three and applying it to our lives, help us to hear what Your Holy Spirit is speaking to us in these words. Help us to find ways to implement this instruction in our lives in a manner that pleases You. We ask this through the Lord Jesus Christ. Amen."

DAY TWENTY-ONE: "Established."

"[1]Therefore when we couldn't stand it any longer, we thought it good to be left behind at Athens alone, [2]and sent Timothy, our brother and God's servant in the Good News of Christ, to establish you, and to comfort you concerning your faith;..." (3:1-2)

God gives us faith to believe Him and then requires us to discipline ourselves to advance in our faith (2 Timothy 2:4-7, 15-26). He gives us the grace to do everything He tells us to do (Titus 2:11-14). Nevertheless, He requires us to do some things. It is not enough to "only believe." Real faith produces fruit in our lives. It makes us change the things that need to be changed. It causes us to become established in the faith. For this, we must engage our mind, body, and soul. God uses His Word and His messengers to establish us in the faith (2 Timothy 2:1). We are designed for growth. God does not save us and leave us. He develops us into productive people of His Kingdom.

CLOSING WORD: **"25Now to Him who is able to establish you according to my gospel and the preaching of Jesus Christ, according to the revelation of the mystery kept secret since the world began 26 but now made manifest, and by the prophetic Scriptures made known to all nations, according to the commandment of the everlasting God, for obedience to the faith— 27 to God, alone wise, *be* glory through Jesus Christ forever. Amen."** (Romans 16:25-26)

PRAYER: "Father, we thank You for calling us to the true faith and granting us true repentance. Strengthen us that we may follow our Lord as faithful disciples and grow in our faith in every way You desire for us. Amen."

DAY TWENTY-TWO: "Comforted."

"1Therefore when we couldn't stand it any longer, we thought it good to be left behind at Athens alone, 2 and sent Timothy, our brother and God's servant in the Good News of Christ, to establish you, and to comfort you concerning your faith;..." (3:1-2)

Real comfort is based on truth. Timothy comforted these believers with God's message of the Good News. The Good News is that God is not holding our sins against us. Jesus has died for our sins. We have been welcomed to come into right relationship with God because of what Jesus has done for us and by God's invitation. He welcomes us into the family of God. The Holy Spirit comforts us by applying God's truth to our hearts and guiding us into a life of following Jesus.

CLOSING WORD: "[16]And I will ask the Father, and He will give you another Comforter (Counselor, Helper, Intercessor, Advocate, Strengthener, and Standby), that He may remain with you forever— [17]The Spirit of Truth, Whom the world cannot receive (welcome, take to its heart), because it does not see Him or know *and* recognize Him. But you know *and* recognize Him, for He lives with you [constantly] and will be in you." (John 14:16-17, AMP)

PRAYER: "Dear Father, thank You for the comfort of the Holy Spirit in my life. Help me to continue to hear and do Your Word. Give me the desire to follow You more closely every day. Amen."

DAY TWENTY-THREE: "Our Only Comfort."

"[1]Therefore when we couldn't stand it any longer, we thought it good to be left behind at Athens alone, [2] and sent Timothy, our brother and God's servant in the Good News of Christ, to establish you, and to comfort you concerning your faith;..." (3:1-2)

The Heidelberg Catechism is an excellent historical resource which God's people can use to help establish themselves in the faith and learn about God's comfort. I highly recommend it. The first question and answer of "LORD'S DAY 1" is, *What is your only comfort in life and death?*

Answer: *That I am not my own, but belong—body and soul, in life and in death—to my faithful Savior, Jesus Christ. He has fully paid for all my sins with his precious blood, and has set me free from the tyranny of the devil. He also watches over me in such a way that not a hair can fall from my head without the will of my Father in heaven; in fact, all things must work together for my salvation. Because I belong to Him, Christ, by His Holy Spirit, assures me of eternal life and makes me wholeheartedly willing and ready from now on to live for Him.*

CLOSING WORD: "But even the hairs of your head are all numbered." (Matthew 10:30)

PRAYER: "Dear Father, You are my life. You are everything to me. May I take comfort in knowing that You care for me and watch my every step. Help me to grow in my faith and be comforted by these truths. Amen."

DAY TWENTY-FOUR: "Triple Knowledge."

"[1]Therefore when we couldn't stand it any longer, we thought it good to be left behind at Athens alone, [2] and sent Timothy, our brother and God's servant in the Good News of Christ, to establish you, and to comfort you concerning your faith;..." (3:1-2)

The second question and answer of the Heidelberg Catechism "LORD'S DAY 1" is also helpful on this subject. It reads, *What must you know to live and die in the joy of this comfort?*

Answer: *Three things: first, how great my sin and misery are; second, how I am set free from all my sins and misery; third, how I am to thank God for such deliverance.*

CLOSING WORD: "This is eternal life, that they should know you, the only true God, and him whom you sent, Jesus Christ." (John 17:3)

PRAYER: "Dear Father, I know my sin has separated me from You. I also know that my Savior has died for me that I may have eternal life. Therefore, I ask You to teach me Your ways. Help me to live as I should for the rest of my life giving thanks to You for the grace You have given to me. Amen."

DAY TWENTY-FIVE: "Testing."

"For this cause I also, when I couldn't stand it any longer, sent that I might know your faith, for fear that by any means the tempter had tempted you, and our labor would have been in vain." (3:5)

Testing comes to all. Many who claim to believe do not endure the testing. The only way I can know how much weight a chain, cable or string can hold is by testing it. As I apply weight (or pressure) to it, its strength becomes evident. As the pressures of life come upon us, our faith is tested, and we discover what is genuine or false in us. God tests us. God allows the devil to tempt and try us. Let us stand the test and prove our faith is genuine.

CLOSING WORD: **"⁶Wherein you greatly rejoice, though now for a little while, if need be, you have been put to grief in various trials, ⁷that the proof of your faith, which is more precious than gold that perishes even though it is tested by fire, may be found to result in praise, glory, and honor at the revelation of Jesus Christ—..."** (1 Peter 1:6-7)

PRAYER: "Dear Father, help me to stand the tests of life and prove my faith to be of the right stuff. In Jesus' name, Amen."

DAY TWENTY-SIX: "Perfecting Faith and Holiness."

"¹⁰Night and day praying exceedingly that we may see your face, and may perfect that which is lacking in your faith?... ¹³ to the end he may establish your hearts blameless in holiness before our God and Father, at the coming of our Lord Jesus with all his saints." (3:10, 13)

We must have enough commitment to God to ask Him to complete what may be lacking in our experience. The shortfall is on our part, not God's. However, it will not fix itself. The spirit is willing, but the flesh is weak. What is lacking manifests itself in our daily lives.

God desires for His people to live holy lives. Holiness is not merely summed-up in dress codes or woman not wearing cosmetics. Holiness is a condition of the heart that manifests itself in our daily lives. Grace is not license to sin. It is the power to live right in this life. Let us look more carefully at our walk. It matters to God.

CLOSING WORD: **"⁸ For you were once darkness, but are now light in the Lord. Walk as children of light, ⁹ for the fruit of the Spirit is in all** goodness and righteousness and truth, [10] proving what is well pleasing to the Lord." (Ephesians 5:8-9)

PRAYER: "Our Father, cleanse our thoughts and help us to adjust our lives to walk before You and the world as children of light. Make us people of prayer and good works. In Your Holy Name, we ask, Amen."

DAY TWENTY-SEVEN: "The Word in Action."

THE WORD FOR TODAY: "[8]For by grace you have been saved through faith, and that not of yourselves; it is the gift of God, [9] not of works, that no one would boast. [10]For we are his workmanship, created in Christ Jesus for good works, which God prepared before that we would walk in them." (Ephesians 2:8-10)

PRAYER: "Gracious Father, I come to You today not in my holiness, but in the holiness of Jesus, my Savior. Show me today ways I can increase in practical holiness day by day as I follow Christ, my Lord. Guide me to see the areas where my faith should be more grounded. Teach me to open up more to the comfort You provide through Your Spirit, and Your Word. In Christ's name, I ask this. Amen."

How I Will Apply the Truth in my Daily Life:
Ways I Will Work Toward Establishing My Faith:

_____

_____

_____

_____

_____

_____

_____

_____

_____

_____

_____

_____

_____

_____

_____

_____

_____

_____

_____

_____

_____

_____

_____

_____

_____

_____

_____

_____

Ways I Will Open Up More To God's Comfort:

_____

_____

_____

_____

_____

_____

_____

_____

_____

_____

_____

_____

_____

_____

_____

_____

_____

_____

_____

How Can I Grow In Holiness?:

_____

_____

_____

_____

_____

_____

_____

_____

_____

_____

_____

_____

_____

_____

_____

_____

_____

_____

_____

_____

_____

_____

THOMAS R. HENDERSHOT

4

EXPECTATION

DAY TWENTY-EIGHT: "Chapter Four"

Today let's familiarize ourselves with chapter four of First Thessalonians. In this chapter, Paul talks about the glorious expectation that we as believers have for the future. We have hope in the second coming of Jesus. I believe we should be excited about what our future holds for us in Christ. Let us go forward now with new expectation in our heart.

CLOSING WORD: **"¹Finally then, brothers, we beg and exhort you in the Lord Jesus, that as you received from us how you ought to walk and to please God, that you abound more and more. ²For you know what instructions we gave you through the Lord Jesus. ³For this is the will of God: your sanctification, that you abstain from sexual immorality, ⁴ that each one of you know how to control his own body in sanctification and honor, ⁵ not in the passion of lust, even as the Gentiles who don't know God; ⁶that no one should take advantage of and wrong a brother or sister in this matter; because the Lord is an** avenger in all these things, as also we forewarned you and testified. [7]For God called us not for uncleanness, but in sanctification. [8]Therefore he who rejects this doesn't reject man, but God, who has also given his Holy Spirit to you. [9]But concerning brotherly love, you have no need that one write to you. For you yourselves are taught by God to love one another, [10]for indeed you do it toward all the brothers who are in all Macedonia. But we exhort you, brothers, that you abound more and more; [11] and that you make it your ambition to lead a quiet life, and to do your own business, and to work with your own hands, even as we instructed you; [12] that you may walk properly toward those who are outside, and may have need of nothing. [13]But we don't want you to be ignorant, brothers, concerning those who have fallen asleep, so that you don't grieve like the rest, who have no hope. [14] For if we believe that Jesus died and rose again, even so God will bring with him those who have fallen asleep in Jesus. [15] For this we tell you by the word of the Lord, that we who are alive, who are left to the coming of the Lord, will in no way precede those who have fallen asleep. [16]For the Lord himself will descend from heaven with a shout, with the voice of the archangel, and with God's trumpet. The dead in Christ will rise first, [17]then we who are alive, who are left, will be caught up together with them in the clouds, to meet the Lord in the air. So we will be with the Lord forever. [18]Therefore comfort one another with these words." (1 Thessalonians 4:1-18)

PRAYER: "Our Father, as we begin learning about the truth of chapter four and applying it to our lives, help us to hear what Your Holy Spirit is speaking to us in these words. Help us to find ways to apply this instruction to our life in a way that pleases You. We ask this through the Lord Jesus Christ. Amen."

DAY TWENTY-NINE: "Growth."

"Finally then, brothers, we beg and exhort you in the Lord Jesus, that as you received from us how you ought to walk and to please God, that you abound more and more." (4:1)

The Bible says a lot about our growing in the Christian life. God's will is for us to grow and be fruitful. We either produce fruit or get pruned. The goal of pruning is that we bear fruit. We may have ups and downs in our spiritual life, but we must learn from all of it, the successes and the failures. We must keep moving forward. We must press toward the mark. We should have lives that bear spiritual fruit. We must grow in our prayer life, Bible study, and other spiritual disciplines. It does not happen automatically. We must deliberately put forth effort and discipline in these areas. We must be intentional.

CLOSING WORD: **"I am the vine. You are the branches. He who remains in me, and I in him, the same bears much fruit, for apart from me you can do nothing."** (John 15:5)

PRAYER: "Oh, Lord, help me to grow in every area of my life, to be fruitful, and to live in a way that is pleasing to You. In the name of Jesus, I ask, Amen."

DAY THIRTY: "Commandments."

"For you know what instructions we gave you through the Lord Jesus." (4:2)

The instructions here are commandments of the Lord. Yes, there are commandments in the new covenant! Most are familiar with the Ten Commandments in the Old Testament (Exodus 20). Many believe that since we are no longer under the sacrificial and ceremonial law of the Old Testament we have no commandments now to keep. They feel that we are in complete liberty. This is not true (John 15:17). The moral law still applies to us (2 Timothy 2:19). God has given many clear guidelines for us to follow (Galatians 5:13-24). Paul shows there are definite limitations to our liberty (1 Corinthians 6:9-20). Believers obey the law of the Spirit (Hebrews 8:10). We do not keep these commandments to earn our salvation. We follow them because we have already received salvation through

Christ. You can do the things a Christian does and not be a Christian, but you cannot be a Christian and not do the things a Christian does. Our *who* influences our *do*. *Who* we are in Christ influences the things we *do*. We love Him, and therefore we keep His commandments (John 14:15).

CLOSING WORD: **"This is my commandment, that you love one another, even as I have loved you."** (John 15:12)

PRAYER: "Oh, Lord. I submit to Your Lordship afresh today. Teach me Your ways and how to keep Your commandments through grace. In the name of the Lord Jesus, I ask this, Amen."

DAY THIRTY-ONE: "Self-Control."

"For this is the will of God: your sanctification,..." (4:3a)

We should not be alarmed by these words. Self-control and sanctification are wonderful words. Sanctification means, "to be set apart for God." It means, "to be holy." The discipline, self-control, and holiness that God demands of us are to help us to walk in true life, not in the ways of death. Sin destroys. It destroys lives and marriages, robs us of our dignity, and tears apart communities and society. God wants us to live, not die. He knows these things will kill, steal, and destroy. He is not trying to keep good things from us (Isaiah 1:18-20). He wants to help us and guard us against many problems. He is offended by sin. We are called to live on a higher level than that of consistently seeking to satisfy our base desires. That is how the world without God lives (1 John 2:15-17). Not His people! Some self-control is a good thing for us (Titus 2:11-14). Practical, sanctified living is good (2 Timothy 2:21).

CLOSING WORD: **"The thief only comes to steal, kill, and destroy. I came that they may have life, and may have it abundantly."** (John 10:10)

PRAYER: "Dear Father, I recognize that the evil one wants me to seek my own desires continually and not to control my body and soul by exercising self-control. Thank You for giving me Your Spirit and Word to help me live out my faith in holiness before You and the world. Amen."

DAY THIRTY-TWO: "Defraud."

"That no one should take advantage of and wrong a brother or sister in this matter; because the Lord is an avenger in all these things, as also we forewarned you and testified." (4:6)

I have heard several folks justify their sinful practices and fleshly or worldly lifestyle by saying, "God told me it was okay." This kind of reasoning is beyond puzzling to me. For an individual to say that certain actions, which God clearly designated as sinful in the scripture, are permitted in their life because God has spoken something different to them from what His Word has already said, is to speak with defraud or by delusion. God does not contradict the clear commandments He has already given in His Word. We must come to God in repentance for our wrong doing. Don't try to rewrite the Bible. Moreover, worse, don't deceive others in this way. It does not put one into the best position with God.

CLOSING WORD: **"Forever, O Lord, Your word is settled in heaven."** (Psalm 119:89, NKJV)

PRAYER: "Oh, Lord, I bow to the authority of Your Word. Please take away every false way from my mind. Renew me with Your Spirit and Your truth. Help me only to hear the voice of the Good Shepherd and not to follow the false voices around me. Amen."

DAY THIRTY-THREE: "The Simple Life."

"But we exhort you, brothers, that you abound more and more; [11]and that you make it your ambition to lead a quiet life, and to do your own business, and to work with your own hands, even as we

instructed you; ¹²that you may walk properly toward those who are
outside, and may have need of nothing." (4:10b-12)

We create many of our own problems. We live in a fast-paced
world, try to do way too many things, and work to have pleasures
rather than to enjoy God with our work and trust Him to provide for
us and our family. We are ambitious for many of the wrong things.
Often we are in other folk's business, both in and outside of the
church. We like juicy gossip. We watch the 24-hour-news-cycle
trying to keep up with all of what's happening around the world. We
are just spread too thin. May God help us to return to a place of
simplicity and real peace, focused on the right things.

CLOSING WORD: "¹³A merry heart makes a cheerful countenance, but
by sorrow of the heart the spirit is broken. ¹⁴ The heart of him who has
understanding seeks knowledge, But the mouth of fools feeds on
foolishness. ¹⁵ All the days of the afflicted *are* evil, But he who is of a
merry heart *has* a continual feast. ¹⁶ Better *is* a little with the fear of the
LORD, Than great treasure with trouble." (Proverbs 15:13-16)

PRAYER: "Oh, Lord, help me to not go a hundred different
directions and miss the life You have planned for me. Teach me to
settle down and discover how to quiet myself in Your presence. Help
me to see the blessing of knowing You are meeting my needs as I live
peacefully through You. Amen."

DAY THIRTY-FOUR: "Asleep in Jesus."

"For this we tell you by the word of the Lord, that we who are alive,
who are left to the coming of the Lord, will in no way precede those
who have fallen asleep." (4:15)

The greatest part of a Christian's life is ahead of him. Death is not
defeat for the real believer. We have hope in death. We know that
for the Chrisitan, it is a falling asleep to this life and awaking in a
better place. Jesus died, rose again and went to heaven. He is the

first-fruits of the resurrection. All true believers will follow His pattern. Death is not the end. It is the gateway to a new beginning. Every person should be prepared to die. Are you? As Christians, we may face death with glorious expectations.

CLOSING WORD: **"Precious in the sight of the LORD is the death of His saints."** (Psalm 116:15, NKJV)

PRAYER: "Oh, Lord, help me to understand that this life is but a vapor of time and that eternity with You is so much better than any of us have ever imagined. Help me not to grieve beyond what You would have me to for those who go ahead of me to that great city. Show me the truth that the eternal realm is far better for the true believer in Christ. Amen."

DAY THIRTY-FIVE: "Great Expectations."

"**16For the Lord himself will descend from heaven with a shout, with the voice of the archangel, and with God's trumpet. The dead in Christ will rise first, 17then we who are alive, who are left, will be caught up together with them in the clouds, to meet the Lord in the air. So we will be with the Lord forever. 18Therefore comfort one another with these words."** (4:16-18)

Christ is coming again. Alleluia! The world will come to an end one day. The believers who have died before He comes will not be left behind. As with death, we must be prepared for His return if we are still living on earth when it happens. This text is not a rescue system designed by God for believers to escape future trouble. It is a glorious eschatological finale before the final judgment. The unbelievers will face a judgment of damnation. Believers will appear before the judgment seat of Christ to receive rewards and to worship Him in heaven for eternity. The eternal heavenly kingdom of God is what awaits believers. Therefore, we look at the end-time encouraged and with great expectations.

CLOSING WORD: "⁵¹Behold, I tell you a mystery. We will not all sleep, but we will all be changed, ⁵²in a moment, in the twinkling of an eye, at the last trumpet. For the trumpet will sound, and the dead will be raised incorruptible, and we will be changed. ⁵³For this perishable body must become imperishable, and this mortal must put on immortality. ⁵⁴But when this perishable body will have become imperishable, and this mortal will have put on immortality, then what is written will happen: "Death is swallowed up in victory." ⁵⁵"Death, where is your sting? Hades, where is your victory?" ⁵⁶The sting of death is sin, and the power of sin is the law. ⁵⁷But thanks be to God, who gives us the victory through our Lord Jesus Christ. ⁵⁸Therefore, my beloved brothers, be steadfast, immovable, always abounding in the Lord's work, because you know that your labor is not in vain in the Lord" (1 Corinthians 15:51-58).

PRAYER: "Oh, Lord, make me ready for Your return. I put my hope in You today. Help me to be steadfast in You and to encourage Your people regardless of the hard times that may come to this earth. You are my Rock in a weary land. My eyes are on You. Make me ready for the future as I worship You, abound in Your work, and wait for the end when You come again. Amen."

DAY THIRTY-SIX: "The Word in Action."

THE WORD FOR TODAY: "Therefore let us also, seeing we are surrounded by so great a cloud of witnesses, lay aside every weight and the sin which so easily entangles us, and let us run with patience the race that is set before us, ²looking to Jesus, the author and perfecter of faith, who for the joy that was set before him endured the cross, despising its shame, and has sat down at the right hand of the throne of God." (Hebrews 12:1-3)

PRAYER: "Father, increase my expectation as I draw closer to You. Develop my faith in You. Teach me to exercise more self-control as I yield to Your Holy Spirit and Your powerful Word. Show me ways to simplify my life and to trust You more fully. In the name of Jesus Christ, I pray. Amen."

How I Will Apply the Truth of This Chapter to my Daily Life:

Ways I Will Work Toward Simplifying My Life:

_____

_____

_____

_____

_____

_____

_____

_____

_____

_____

_____

_____

_____

_____

_____

_____

_____

_____

_____

_____

_____

Areas in Which I Want to Develop More Self-Control:

_____

_____

_____

_____

_____

_____

_____

_____

_____

_____

_____

_____

_____

My Expectation is Increasing in These Ways:

_____

_____

_____

_____

_____

_____

_____

_____

_____

_____

_____

_____

_____

_____

_____

_____

_____

_____

_____

5

ENLIGHTENMENT

DAY THIRTY-SEVEN: "Chapter Five"

Today let's familiarize ourselves with chapter five of First Thessalonians. In this chapter, Paul teaches believers some things about practical holiness and spiritual alertness. We certainly need this enlightenment in our time.

CLOSING WORD: "¹But concerning the times and the seasons, brothers, you have no need that anything be written to you. ²For you yourselves know well that the day of the Lord comes like a thief in the night. ³For when they are saying, "Peace and safety," then sudden destruction will come on them, like birth pains on a pregnant woman; and they will in no way escape. ⁴But you, brothers, aren't in darkness, that the day should overtake you like a thief. ⁵You are all children of light, and children of the day. We don't belong to the night, nor to darkness, ⁶ so then let's not sleep, as the rest do, but let's watch and be sober. ⁷For those who sleep, sleep in the night, and those who are drunk are drunk in the night. ⁸But let us, since we belong to the day, be sober, putting on the breastplate of faith and love, and, for a helmet, the hope of salvation. [9]For God didn't appoint us to wrath, but to the obtaining of salvation through our Lord Jesus Christ, [10]who died for us, that, whether we wake or sleep, we should live together with him. [11]Therefore exhort one another, and build each other up, even as you also do. [12]But we beg you, brothers, to know those who labor among you, and are over you in the Lord, and admonish you, [13]and to respect and honor them in love for their work's sake. Be at peace among yourselves. [14]We exhort you, brothers, admonish the disorderly, encourage the faint-hearted, support the weak, be patient toward all. [15]See that no one returns evil for evil to anyone, but always follow after that which is good, for one another, and for all. [16]Rejoice always. [17]Pray without ceasing. [18]In everything give thanks, for this is the will of God in Christ Jesus toward you. [19]Don't quench the Spirit. [20]Don't despise prophesies. [21]Test all things, and hold firmly that which is good. [22]Abstain from every form of evil. [23]May the God of peace himself sanctify you completely. May your whole spirit, soul, and body be preserved blameless at the coming of our Lord Jesus Christ. [24]He who calls you is faithful, who will also do it. [25]Brothers, pray for us. [26]Greet all the brothers with a holy kiss. [27]I solemnly command you by the Lord that this letter be read to all the holy brothers. [28]The grace of our Lord Jesus Christ be with you. Amen." (1 Thessalonians 5:1-28)

PRAYER: "Our Father, as we begin learning about the truth of chapter five and applying it to our lives, help us to hear what Your Holy Spirit is speaking to us in these words. Help us to find the places and methods to apply this instruction to our lives in ways which are pleasing to You. We ask this through the Lord Jesus Christ. Amen."

DAY THIRTY-EIGHT: "Times and Seasons."

"[1]But concerning the times and the seasons, brothers, you have no need that anything be written to you. [2]For you yourselves know well that the day of the Lord comes like a thief in the night. [3]For when they are saying, "Peace and safety," then sudden destruction will come on them, like birth pains on a pregnant woman; and they will in no way escape." (5:1-3)

As we grow in our relationship with God, we learn the importance of recognizing times and seasons in our lives and our world. Here Paul is specifically referring to the times and seasons as it relates to the Day of the Lord. The Day of the Lord is a theme that reaches back into the Old Testament referring to God's judgment. Therefore, Paul is continuing the theme of the final days and resurrection he was talking about at the end of chapter four. He is telling these believers they need not worry about missing out on the resurrection as do the unbelievers. The unbelievers go on through life and miss out believing that everything is peaceful and secure. Paul had apparently taught the believers about this while he was there with them.

False prophets in the Old Testament promised peace and safety. The true prophets told of God's impending judgment upon evil doers (Jeremiah 23:17, Amos 5:18-19). The true believers must stay alert to the Times and Seasons but not try to guess the dates. Our hope is in Christ, not in predictions (Matthew 24:23, 36 and Acts 1:6-8).

CLOSING WORD: "For everything there is a season, and a time for every purpose under heaven:..." (Ecclesiastes 3:1)

PRAYER: "Oh, Lord, keep me focused on the right aspects of Your Second Advent. Don't allow me to be carried away with predictions about the Day of the Lord, but rather teach me to rest in the finished work of Christ for my salvation and trust You with the things that concern the end. Ready me to meet You, dear Lord. Amen."

DAY THIRTY-NINE: "Wake Up!"

"So then let's not sleep, as the rest do, but let's watch and be sober. 7For those who sleep, sleep in the night,..." (5:6-7a)

Trusting God with the final days does not mean we live in any way our flesh dictates. No, it means we live soberly and watchfully. We are aware of the evil around us. We are not asleep to the darkness that confronts our world. We are worshiping, working, and waiting. We are focused on the right things. We are busy telling others about the love of Christ and the rule of God. We are not trying to predict final things, but we also do not stand around with our heads in the sand. We are ready for Christ's return. We live in this readiness both watchfully and soberly. We live in expectation and hope. We are an enlightened people.

CLOSING WORD: **"Be sober and self-controlled. Be watchful. Your adversary, the devil, walks around like a roaring lion, seeking whom he may devour."** (1 Peter 5:8)

PRAYER: "Our Father, we thank You for the plan You have for the future. We thank You for giving us an awareness of the final days. Keep us alert and productive for the kingdom of God. Help us to be aware of the evil as it escalates in our day. However, help us to use this enlightenment to ready ourselves and others for Your Son's return, for it is in His name we pray, Amen."

DAY FORTY: "Build Each Other Up."

"Therefore exhort one another, and build each other up, even as you also do." (5:11)

Let us look at the times around us and the problems of this earth and realize that but for the grace of God we would surely be destroyed. We are God's people and must encourage each other. Look for ways to build up other believers you know. Encourage your brother and sister in Christ. We have a unique purpose in this life and an extraordinary destiny ahead of us. We should warn, admonish, encourage and pray for each other. We need one another.

WORSHIPING, WORKING, AND WAITING

Some attention and encouragement will go a long way in the life of somebody you know.

CLOSING WORD: **"Let the word of Christ dwell in you richly; in all wisdom teaching and admonishing one another with psalms, hymns, and spiritual songs, singing with grace in your heart to the Lord."** (Colossians 3:16)

PRAYER: "Dear Lord, help me to encourage and build up the believers I know. You have put us together in this time and place for good reasons. Help us to be the family of God on earth and help each other. Open my eyes to see who I can be a blessing to in the upcoming days. Amen."

DAY FORTY-ONE: "Rejoice."

"Rejoice always." (5:16)

We began this adventure through this letter of Paul emphasizing three words: Worship, Work, and Wait. In this verse, Paul takes us back to the theme of worship. The next several verses call attention to some spiritual disciplines that will help every believer in their walk with Christ. This is a part of our working and waiting too. Let us learn from these insights and apply them to our lives.

Rejoice! Many believers know this admonition but seldom find themselves doing it. Do it! Don't wait until you figure out how to properly do it before you begin. God will lead you and help you. Your part is to do it. Start today.

Notice the word, "always" above. This is referring to more than Sunday morning. It is talking about more than when things go well. It is a lifestyle. It is an attitude. It is a habit. Again, it starts by doing it. Get started now.

CLOSING WORD: **"Rejoice in the Lord always. Again I will say, rejoice!"** (Philippians 4:4, MEV) **"This is the day that the LORD has made;**

let us rejoice and be glad in it." (Psalm 118:24, ESV)

PRAYER: "Heavenly Father, forgive me for not rejoicing with the intensity and frequency of which You have instructed me. Remind me of this commandment throughout my days. Teach me to rejoice at all times and for all things. I rejoice before You now! Amen."

DAY FORTY-TWO: "Pray."

"Pray without ceasing." (5:17) **"Brothers, pray for us."** (5:25)

Christians pray. You can pray and not be a Christian, but you cannot be a Christian and not pray. Again, Paul emphasized frequency here. Don't just wait for times of formal expression. Pray all day long. If you will pray in the morning and set your mind and heart toward heaven, you can continue the conversation all day long. Try to make a habit of praying the Lord's Prayer as You drink your morning beverage or before you get out of bed every day. After a short while, it will become a habit. (Matthew 6:9-13, Luke 18:1-6).

Pray for others in your life. Pray for the fellow believers you know. God works through prayer. Do it much and do it often. In fact, why not start a continual conversation with God today and never stop it?

CLOSING WORD: **"Continue in prayer, and be watchful with thanksgiving, ³while praying also for us, that God would open to us a door of utterance to speak the mystery of Christ, for which I am also in chains, ⁴that I may reveal it clearly, as I ought to speak."** (Colossians 4:2-4)

PRAYER: "Our Father, I pray now that You will bless and help my brothers and sisters in Christ. Give my pastor an open door of utterance to preach Your Word. Bless and help all the people of my church. Bless and encourage Your people everywhere, as I join in with believers around the world now and pray the prayer Your Son,

Jesus, taught us to pray, saying: *'Our Father which art in heaven, Hallowed be thy name. [10]Thy kingdom come, Thy will be done in earth, as it is in heaven. [11]Give us this day our daily bread. [12]And forgive us our debts, as we forgive our debtors. [13]And lead us not into temptation, but deliver us from evil: For thine is the kingdom, and the power, and the glory, forever. Amen'"* (Matthew 6:9b-13, KJV).

DAY FORTY-THREE: "Giving Thanks."

"In everything give thanks, for this is the will of God in Christ Jesus toward you." (5:18)

On day three we talked about, "Cultivating a Lifestyle of Thanksgiving." To give thanks in everything is the same idea. Some folks are never thankful. Some are seldom thankful. Some are generally thankful. Paul tells us to be continually thankful. Make it a lifestyle. He instructs us to give thanks in every situation. Make this spiritual discipline a part of your life every day. It is transforming.

CLOSING WORD: **"Oh give thanks to the LORD, for he is good; for his steadfast love endures forever!"** (Psalm 118:1, ESV)

PRAYER: "Lord, I give thanks to You today regardless of my situation. I know You are good and merciful. Help me to keep my eyes on You and be thankful each and every day through Jesus Christ my Savior. Amen."

DAY FORTY-FOUR: "The Holy Spirit."

"Don't quench the Spirit." (5:19)

The Holy Spirit indwells every true believer. This means He is in us and with us in every situation and in everything we do. He came to help us to follow God and to lead us and guide us. However, He is holy. We can offend Him by the things we say and do. We can grieve Him. We can quench His flow in our lives by not yielding to Him. He is a gentleman. He does not force His way on us. Therefore, we must be conscious of His presence and treat Him with the respect and reverence due to Him as God.

We should not attribute every thought we get as coming from the Holy Spirit. However, we should not think that He is not still speaking into our lives either. We live in a real world and need real-world help. Therefore, we must open our hearts and minds to His leading and guiding and receive the help He offers us. His goal is to draw us closer to Christ. We must not disobey His admonition to us. Let us walk wholeheartedly in His ways.

CLOSING WORD: "**⁵For those who live according to the flesh set their minds on the things of the flesh, but those who live according to the Spirit set their minds on the things of the Spirit. ⁶ For to set the mind on the flesh is death, but to set the mind on the Spirit is life and peace. ⁷ For the mind that is set on the flesh is hostile to God, for it does not submit to God's law; indeed, it cannot. ⁸Those who are in the flesh cannot please God. ⁹ You, however, are not in the flesh but in the Spirit, if in fact the Spirit of God dwells in you. Anyone who does not have the Spirit of Christ does not belong to him.**" (Romans 8:5-9)

PRAYER: "Father, we are indeed a needy people. We need Your help every day. Help each of us, O' Lord, to not quench the voice of Your Holy Spirit within us and His leading and guiding in our lives. Teach us to draw from His presence the strength we need to live for You in this troubled world. Amen."

DAY FORTY-FIVE: "Prophecy."

"**²⁰Don't despise prophesies. ²¹Test all things, and hold firmly that which is good.**" (5:20-21)

The concept of prophecy for today is a controversial subject. First, no one is rewriting the Bible. It is complete. However, this does not mean that God is not still presently leading His people in ways that are consistent with the overall revelation He has already given in His Word.

A prophecy is words. We live by words. We are taught, we are guided by, and we communicate through words. Therefore, it is unreasonable to think God does not still communicate to us through words. We need guidance for today. He is able to give us the words we need in various ways. He is a God who speaks, not a dumb idol (1 Corinthians 12:1-3).

However, when we start down this line of thinking it is obvious that most of what folks claim is a prophecy today is not a prophecy at all. Often, individuals share many human inspired ideas. This can be discouraging for us. However, the instruction for "Day Forty-Five" is for us to not treat the subject of prophecy with contempt. "**Don't despise prophesies.**" There are many false prophets (1 John 4:1). Nevertheless, this does not mean there are not some folks speaking forth prophetic truth also. We must not throw the baby out with the bathwater. You cannot have a counterfeit unless there is also a real that exists.

At a minimum, we must treat with the highest regard every word God has given us in the scripture. We should also believe that God is still speaking in our time (Romans 8:14, Revelation 3:22). It is not creating new scripture. It is shining the light of God on His Word and our path for us to see the truth in our time. It must be completely consistent with everything else He has ever said. I believe He can get the message to us we need if we are open to hearing from Him.

CLOSING WORD: **"Follow after love, and earnestly desire spiritual gifts, but especially that you may prophesy."** (1 Corinthians 14:1)

PRAYER: "Oh, Lord, help me to hear Your voice in my life. Help me to be Your voice in the lives of others. Guard me against every false voice as I incline my ear to You. Let me be a lamb who hears my Shepherd's voice. Amen."

DAY FORTY-SIX: "If It Looks Bad,..."

"Abstain from every form of evil." (5:22)

Many professing Christians seem to have an attitude of, "how much sinning can I get away with?" "What are the limits?" This attitude reveals a much deeper issue. It shows a commitment to self-satisfaction rather than to pleasing God. Which way do you lean?

Many professing believers say that grace is all that matters. This is true but must be applied correctly. Grace does not mean that I get to sin all I want and expect God to overlook my sin and forgive me and continually bless me regardless of my disobedience. Grace teaches us to abstain from evil (Titus 2:11-12). God loves us. He wants us free from sin. He knows sin will destroy our lives.

Look at it like a normal responsible parent would look at drugs and their child. The father is not trying to stop the kid from having fun by telling them to abstain from drugs. He is attempting to save the child from misery and death. God views sin and His children much the same way we as parents look at drugs and our kids. As God's children, let us abstain from anything that appears evil and let us seek to please God, our heavenly Father and escape many of the potential miseries of this life.

Abstaining from the appearance of evil is like the guardrail on a highway with a steep cliff. The guardrail is not the cliff, and if you touch it you will not die, but it is a barrier that reveals that we are very close to imminent danger. Ask God to help you to erect some guardrails (boundaries) in your life.

CLOSING WORD: **"Let the words of my mouth and the meditation of my heart be acceptable in Your sight, O Lord, my strength and my Redeemer."** (Psalm 19:14, MEV)

PRAYER: "Oh, Lord, my strength and my Redeemer. Show me the things I need to draw back away from in my life. Draw me closer to

You in unreserved obedience, in Christ, my Savior's name, I plead. Help me to not desire the things of this world that will destroy me. Help me to establish good and helpful boundaries in my life. Holy Spirit, guide me in the paths of righteousness for Your name's sake. Lord, I want to please You. Strengthen me now. Amen."

DAY FORTY-SEVEN: "Total Transformation."

"²³May the God of peace himself sanctify you completely. May your whole spirit, soul, and body be preserved blameless at the coming of our Lord Jesus Christ. ²⁴ He who calls you is faithful, who will also do it." (5:23-24)

Let us be those people who are seeking and expecting total transformation. When God saves us, He puts new life within us. Our dead spirits come alive. As we grow, we are renewed in our minds. In the resurrection, our bodies will receive a total change. Consequently, we are saved, in the state of being saved, and we are yet to be saved. In our spirits, we are indeed changed. In our souls, we are being transformed. Our bodies await the total change of the resurrection. We can trust God to bring about this total transformation. He will complete what He has started. May we present ourselves as living sacrifices before Him and seek His total transformation in our lives.

CLOSING WORD: "I urge you therefore, brothers, by the mercies of God, that you present your bodies as a living sacrifice, holy, and acceptable to God, which is your reasonable service of worship. ² Do not be conformed to this world, but be transformed by the renewing of your mind, that you may prove what is the good and acceptable and perfect will of God." (Romans 12:1-2, MEV)

PRAYER: "Father, I submit to You now. I give myself over to You and Your will in my life. Take me and transform me into the image of Your Son. Help me to deny the flesh, the world, and the devil.

Apply Your Word and Spirit to every part of my life. I present myself to You, in Jesus' name. Amen."

DAY FORTY-EIGHT: "Some Final Words."

"**26 Greet all the brothers with a holy kiss. 27 I solemnly command you by the Lord that this letter be read to all the holy brothers.**" (5:26-27)

As believers, I think we hinder the advancement of the gospel in our world through our lack of cooperation with each other. Love has an attraction to it. If we would show more love and compassion to one another others would see and know that we are the true disciples of Jesus. Instead of responding with gossip, let us bless our fellow believers. Instead of drawing back from fellowship, let us draw closer to each other. Instead of being mean-spirited, let us hug our fellow saints. What joy this would bring to God and what peace it would release in our lives! May we obey God's commands through His leaders among us and be blessed!

CLOSING WORD: "**19We love him, because he first loved us. 20 If a man says, "I love God," and hates his brother, he is a liar; for he who doesn't love his brother whom he has seen, how can he love God whom he has not seen? 21 This commandment we have from him, that he who loves God should also love his brother.**" (1 John 4:19-21)

PRAYER: "Dear God, forgive me for all the times when I did not express or display the kind of love and support I should have to my fellow believers, Your children. Help me to share the love You have put into my heart with others more freely and more sincerely thus confirming that I am indeed one of Your children and am doing that which is pleasing in Your sight. In Your name I ask. Amen."

DAY FORTY-NINE: "Grace Bestowed and Proclaimed."

"**The grace of our Lord Jesus Christ be with you. Amen.**" (5:28)

May the God of grace bless you and keep you. He loves you and has called you to follow Him. That is why you have desired to read this book and perform these spiritual disciplines. He has called you by His grace into His grace. He will empower you to do what is pleasing in His sight. As you yield to Him, it is a much more rewarding journey. You are called to worship, to work, and to wait. May you do this fully by His grace. Amen... so be it!

CLOSING WORD: **"Now, brothers, I entrust you to God, and to the word of his grace, which is able to build up, and to give you the inheritance among all those who are sanctified."** (Acts 20:32)

PRAYER: "Oh, Father, thank You for the grace You have displayed in my life. I ask You to continue to build up this grace in my life as You work Your sanctifying power within me. I stand on the Word of grace today. Release me from bondage and move me into greater purpose and power as I worship You, work in Your kingdom and wait for Your Son's return. Amen and Amen."

DAY FIFTY: "The Word in Action."

THE WORD FOR TODAY: **"2 Grace to you and peace be multiplied in the knowledge of God and of Jesus our Lord, 3 seeing that his divine power has granted to us all things that pertain to life and godliness, through the knowledge of him who called us by his own glory and virtue; 4 by which he has granted to us his precious and exceedingly great promises; that through these you may become partakers of the divine nature, having escaped from the corruption that is in the world by lust. 5 Yes, and for this very cause adding on your part all diligence, in your faith supply moral excellence; and in moral excellence, knowledge; 6 and in knowledge, self-control; and in self-control patience; and in patience godliness; 7 and in godliness brotherly affection; and in brotherly affection, love. 8For if these things are yours and abound, they make you to be not idle nor unfruitful to the** knowledge of our Lord Jesus Christ. [9]For he who lacks these things is blind, seeing only what is near, having forgotten the cleansing from his old sins. [10]Therefore, brothers, be more diligent to make your calling and election sure. For if you do these things, you will never stumble. [11] For thus you will be richly supplied with the entrance into the eternal Kingdom of our Lord and Savior, Jesus Christ." (2 Peter 1:2-11)

PRAYER: "Father, show me ways I can build-up my brothers and sisters around me. Teach me to pray. Help me to hear Your voice clearly in my life. Guard me against every false voice and tune my spiritual ears to hear what Your Spirit is saying to the churches. I ask this in faith in my Savior and in His name. Amen."

How I Will Apply the Truth in my Daily Life:
Ways I Will Work Toward Building Up My Fellow Believers:

_____

_____

_____

_____

_____

_____

_____

_____

_____

_____

_____

_____

_____

_____

_____

_____

_____

_____

_____

_____

_____

_____

_____

_____

_____

_____

How is God Helping Me to Pray (For What Things?):

_____

_____

_____

_____

_____

_____

_____

_____

_____

_____

_____

_____

_____

_____

_____

_____

_____

_____

_____

_____

_____

_____

_____

_____

_____

_____

THOMAS R. HENDERSHOT

In What Ways Am I Becoming More Aware of the Holy Spirit's Presence?:

_____
_____
_____
_____
_____
_____
_____
_____
_____
_____
_____
_____
_____
_____
_____
_____
_____
_____
_____
_____
_____
_____
_____
_____
_____
_____
_____
_____
_____

OTHER BOOKS AVAILABLE AT:

Createspace: http://www.createspace.com   (Go to **STORE** drop box and type in name — "Thomas Hendershot")
Amazon: http://www.amazon.com
Amazon Author's Page: http://www.amazon.com/Thomas-R.-Hendershot
Barnes and Noble: http://www.barnesandnoble.com/
Alibris: http://www.alibris.com/booksearch

Possessing the Land
Ministry to the Sick
Guarding Your Heart and Mind
Psalms, Hymns and Spiritual Songs
Saints in Strange Situations
Doors

Secrets of the Blessed Life Series
The Blessing in the Valley (Psalm 84)
Covenant Confidence (Psalm 25)
The Blessing of Shamar (Psalm 121)
Samach (Psalm 16)

Insights for Daily Living
Worshipping, Working, and Waiting
Worthy of the Kingdom

Evangelical Essentials Series
Book One: The Name and Nature of God

Pastoral Perspectives Series
Book One: Spiritual Wisdom for the Church
I & II Thessalonians

Made in the USA
Middletown, DE
21 April 2024

53260717R00042